Emma May Buckingham

Pearl

A Centennial Poem

Emma May Buckingham

Pearl
A Centennial Poem

ISBN/EAN: 9783744711128

Printed in Europe, USA, Canada, Australia, Japan

Cover: Foto ©Thomas Meinert / pixelio.de

More available books at **www.hansebooks.com**

A CENTENNIAL POEM.

BY

EMMA MAY BUCKINGHAM,

AUTHOR OF "A SELF-MADE WOMAN."

"All love is sweet—given or returned.
Common as *light* is love,
And its familiar voice
Wearies not ever."—SHELLEY.

NEW YORK:

S. R. WELLS & COMPANY, PUBLISHERS,

737 BROADWAY.

1877.

To

ALL WHO HAVE ENCOURAGED ME TO PERSEVERE IN MY
LITERARY LABORS,

I Dedicate

THIS VOLUME.

CONTENTS.

I.

PEARL MALLEY.

" 'THE world is a sea of snow-white daisies,
  I walk knee-deep in the level tide;
Slowly I wade, and the fragrant billows
  Part at my coming on either side,

" 'Make me a path through their lovely sweetness,
  See, in my wake, like a track of foam,
Pallid they lie with their fair heads drooping,
  Sadly marking my pathway home.' "

Sang the fair " Margarié, Pearl of the Valley,"
  Margaret Malley, a girl of sixteen,
Heiress of all the rich lands of Lord Malley,
  " Pride of the Hall," where she reigned like a
    queen—

Trilling so sweetly the beautiful numbers,
  Culling the blossoming plants by the way;
Plucking the berries that crimson'd the meadows;
  Fairer than gold-hearted daisies, or day.

Cheeks on which lilies and roses contended ;
    Recklessly wantoned the breeze with her hair,
Tresses, with hazel and amber gleams blended ;
    Eyes brown and lovely, a brow wide and fair.

Even her walk was perfection of motion ;
    Lithe was her form as the willows that dream
Over the streamlet that hastes to the ocean,—
    Thoughts pure as lilies that float on the stream.

Sorrow and pain were unknown to Pearl Malley ;
    Never was bobolink freer from care ;
Love and Dame Fortune—the Elves of the
    Valley—
    Guarded her childhood and girlhood so fair.

No fancies idle, of love or of lover,
    Stirred the calm deeps of her nature serene,
Either, while wading through pink - hooded
    clover,
    Or the sweet ferns, 'neath the Park's leafy
    screen.

II.

PAUL LEIGHTON.

STRETCHED on the fern-tufted bank of the lakelet,
  Sketching the shadows in idle delight,
Tracing the delicate veins of the leaflet,
  Building air-castles as roomy, as bright

As mansions of bliss in Poe's distant Aidenn—
  Leighton, the famous young artist, for hours
'Waiting the tardy return of the maiden—
  "A Hebe," he called her, "crowned with June
    flowers."

Ah, Lady Margaret! Give me kind greeting!
  Can it be Pearl?" and the laughing eyes
    gleamed;
Dear little Margarié! Of this, our meeting,
  While I was absent, how often I dreamed!"

Pearl, I have come to the Hall, for the season;
  Your father and mine are old schoolmates.
    You see

(11)

They've sent me to find you—this is the reason
    I recognized you as the child Margarié,

"Whom, ten years agone, I petted and fondled.
    Pearl, how you laughed—when the tall, awk-
        ward boy
Gave you a ride on his shoulder, or trundled
    Your wee, baby-carriage—and shouted for joy.'

Blushes as red as the lush, wild strawberry
    Stained her pure cheek as she held out her
        hand;
Bright was her welcoming smile; glad and merry
    And sweet her young voice, the words at com-
        mand.

Thus, did she graciously welcome Paul Leighton
    There 'neath the shade of the lindens so tall;
And, while he talked, how her face flushed and
        brightened;
    Beautiful Margaret, queen of the Hall.

III.

A SUMMER.

OH, what a summer of bloom and of beauty !
  Couleur de rose was earth, ocean, and air,
Ay, a new Eden ; and *love* was but *duty ;*
  Never was season to lovers as fair.

Day after day, through the sweet summer
        weather,
  Over the Manor they strolled side by side ;
Sat by the ocean, for long hours together,
  Watching the ebbing and incoming tide.

Paul, in the gloaming, new songs kindly taught
        her ;
  Paul, in art studies, directed her mind ;
Read the best poems to father and daughter ;
  Never was brother or teacher more kind.

"Sit for your portrait," he said, "my Queen Mar-
        g'ret ;
  Or to the terrace, come, dear Lady Pearl,

And study the clouds," or "rare golden sunset,"
But *Paul* only studied the gold of her curls.

Oh, what a dream of sweet love to the maiden!
Never had lover a treasure so rare ;
Surely, *to love* was the soul's destined Aidenn ;
Never to youth looked the future more fair!

But, the dear summer gave place to October,
Monarch so haughty, so heartless and bold ;
Trailing o'er meadows his robes brown and sober,
Painting the forests with crimson and gold.

And, with the season, their bright dream was over;
Back to her studies Pearl Malley had fled ;
Paul was, again, in the Old World a rover,
Sighing for days that forever were dead.

IV.

PEARL.

GONE without saying "good-night!"
  Gone with the summer so blest;
Gone with my girl-heart so light—
  Gone with his love unconfessed.

Oh, had he bade me "good-bye!"
  Or, in warm clasp, held my hand;
And, with kind words, or a sigh,
  Made my torn heart understand

LOVE urged him longer to stay,
  But, the stern Fates bade him go;
That Duty brooked no delay—
  I could have borne it, I know.

Though I must crush this first grief—
  Death of my love and my youth—
Still, it will be some relief
  From him to hear all the truth.

For, such a tender "good-bye"
Soon he will write me, I'm sure,
That, through long years I shall try
Patiently, all to endure.

V.

PAUL.

YES, the summer dream is over;
   Back to study, work, and care;
Back to wed Lulena Snover
   Tall, and dark, with midnight hair;

Flashing eyes, whose dusky splendor
   Soon will pierce my secret through;
Though I play the lover tender,
   She will read my eyes untrue.

Oh, to hold my brown-eyed beauty
   For one moment to my heart!
Oh, to kiss her lips! but duty
   Bids me hastily depart.

Bids me go like thief at midnight—
   Steal away before the day—
Fearful that her smile and daylight
   Will persuade me still to stay.

(17)

To sweet Pearl, I'll write a letter,
  Show her all my sad, sad heart;
And, convince the child, 'tis better
  That thus suddenly we part.

Or, a message I will send her;
  For, she knows no more of love
Than the stars, whose dreamy splendor
  Calmly lights the sea above.

True and artless is Pearl Malley,
  Pure her life, from care as free
As the lilies of the valley,
  Or the daisies on the lea.

I have sought to win her never;
  Did not mean to give her pain;
But, to Lulu, all endeavor
  To be true, has been in vain.

Yes, my summer idyl's over—
  Dream of bliss too sweet to last—
I will wed Lulena Snover
  And redeem my fickle Past.

VI.

NO LETTERS.

WRESTLING alone with my sorrow;
  Weary of friends and home;
Hoping, in vain, that the morrow
  Letters will bring from Rome.

Veiling my anguish and smiling
  Gayly when friends are near;
Memory often beguiling
  With music once so dear.

Avoiding the "Woodbine Bowers,"
  "The Ramble" in the dell;
Paul's favorite books and flowers,
  The songs he loved so well—

Colors and games, once a pleasure
  To us, aside I've laid
As they fold away the treasures
  And garments of the dead.

(19)

Silently, patiently hiding
　My grief from all at home ;
Wearily waiting for tidings—
　Longing abroad to roam.

VII.

LULENA.

I'VE wedded the peerless Lulena,
  But, in our luxurious home
In view of the ruined arena
  Where Gladiators of old Rome
Once fought with wild beasts, I am waging
  A conflict e'en fiercer than they;
Or even the fiery floods raging
  In yon tireless crater to-day.

Lulena molds deftly in plaster
  And chisels from marble, so cold,
Such breathing creations her masters
  Must look to their laurels of old.
As grand as the Psyches she fashions,
  As cold as her Junos of clay;
"Loves Art with wild fervor and passion—
  A queen among women," they say.

As wise as Aspasia's Lulena,
  Or yet, as the fair Zobeide;

Gifts rare as De Stael's grand *Corinna*
   Of mind, not of *heart*, has my bride.
A war with my love and my duty
   I'm waging to-day—ah, Lulene!
Your genius, proud name, fame and beauty,
   I'd barter for Pearl, my soul's queen.

For, when amid ruins we dally—
   Or Vatican's art treasures old,
Instead of my bride, 'tis Pearl Malley
   With tresses of amber and gold,
Anear.   Or, beneath the acacias
   On blooming *Campagna* I see
Thy brown eyes, Oh, queen of the daisies!
   Tho' Lulu's are smiling on me.

The hair I caress with glad seeming,
   The lips that by mine are oft pressed;
Are Lulene's; yet, in fancy, I'm dreaming
   With Margaret's head on my breast.
A *lie* I am living, for hourly
   Her face, young and sweet, comes between
My own and my bride's—God forgive me
   For loving *her* more than Lulene!

VIII.

TIDINGS.

YES, I see, I have made a mistake;
  That Paul never has loved me, I own;
What an error for maiden to make!
  Yet the fault was not his—mine alone.
I am sadder, I ween, than poor Eve
  When she tearfully heard the command:
'Thou this beautiful garden must leave;"
  And with Adam went out hand in hand.

For, his love went with Eve, when exiled
  From the bowers of " Eden the Blest;"
It illumined the deserts so wild—
  Pain was pleasure, and labor sweet rest.
No more desolate, dreary, and dark
  Looked the sea-covered world to the eight
Sailing over the flood in the Ark
  Than to me looks my own loveless fate.

Though the homes, that once gladdened their
      lives,
  With their dead, lay beneath oceans vast;

They were blessed with their husbands and
    wives,
  And with pleasure, remembered the past.
Ah, how weak the romances have proved!
    When compared with my own, how inane;
All their heroines love, are beloved—
    Ever true to each other remain.

By Leander, young Hero was loved;
  With Pyramus, fair Thisbe was blest;
Juliet and Romeo—unmoved
    I can read—for I covet their rest.

Even lost Eurydice, I've read,
  Was beloved by Orpheus, the brave,
For he entered the "*Shades of the Dead*"
    To redeem her from Death and the grave.

Oh, my dream was too precious to last!
    I must waken and bury my dead;
God forgive me for dalliance past
    With my grief, and the joys that have fled

I will put this deep sorrow away,
  And, with laughter, my agony hide;
For Paul Leighton is married, they say,
    To Lulena, a proud Southern bride.

I will strangle my weakness and pain,
　Gay and happy endeavor to be;
Though, the future, oh, never again
　May the sweet bells of hope ring for me!
And, to-morrow, I'll journey from home
　With my father, remote lands to see;
Where, for years, we shall probably roam—
　For the Hall is distasteful to me.

IX.

A RETROSPECT.

YES, seven years have passed away—
It seems a century, to-day,
Since, looking backward, through the years
Of sun and shade, of joy or tears,
I see a far-off rosy June
With Nature's voices all in tune.

A maiden dancing o'er the lea—
A snow-white, fragrant, blooming sea—
And, through that golden summer, rife
With bliss that comes but *once in life*,
I hear her footsteps, light as air,
Her youthful voice so free from care;

Then, joyous laughter floats away
Into the misty autumn gray,
Full soon, a grief, too deep for tears,
Threatens to darken all her years;
Till He, who calmed the stormy sea,
Gives peace of mind to Margarie.

(27)

Then, years of travel hurry past—
Years fraught with culture, till, at last,
Weary of study, absence, change,
Of suitors too—who think it strange
" The lovely heiress "—" child of song "—
" Remains in single bliss so long; "

With joy she turns like Noäh's dove,
And seeks home's restful Ark of love.
There, cheering her loved sire with song,
She finds the joys departed long
From olden haunts and wildwood bowers,
And, lives again, with birds and flowers.

X.

AFTER SEVEN YEARS.

THE wintry wind moans in the pines,
The snow sifts through the trellised vines,
Across the porch, the dead leaves fall,
And, o'er the threshold of the Hall;
While, in the distance, Leighton sees
An open grave, beneath the trees.

Within a chamber white and cold,
A shrouded form—withered and old
The face, but filled with heaven's peace,
As thankful for the soul's release.
The pain Lord Malley many years
Has borne, is o'er.   What room for tears?

Yet, mutely, sadly standing there
Tearless and pale, her curling hair
Enveloping, like wavy gold,
Her form—clad in the sable folds
Of mourning, mockery grief,
Sad outward garb, and no relief;

The Lady Pearl, the last of all
The Malleys of this ancient Hall—
Where ancestors their wassail songs
Had sung, a century agone,
He sees—but grown more fair and tall
Is " Margaret, Queen of the Hall."

.   .   .   .   .

Soon by her side, she saw him stand
Smiling and holding out his hand,
As famishing for look or word
Of kindness.
       " Margaret, I heard
The heavy tidings on my way
To visit *him.* Give welcome, pray."
" My father loved him—for *his* sake
His child, again Paul's hand will take;"
She thought, and said : " Ah, truant Paul!
For *his* sake, welcome to the Hall."
Cold as the corse, the hand she gave,
Formal and few her words, and grave,
Then silently she kissed her dead
And turned away, with noiseless tread,
And left the artist standing there
In mute surprise, almost despair.
Yes, anger fierce, to think that she
Should treat him thus, so cruelly.

Paul, at a later hour, that day,
When all she loved was laid away

Beneath the beeches, grand and tall,
Which stood like sentries near the Hall,
Wrote, for she would not see him : " Fair,
' Queen Margaret,'
          Oh, Pearl most rare
Of womankind ! I've come, at last—
To win your love—redeem the past.

   `   •   •   •   •   •

" My wife in classic Rome to-night
Sleeps 'neath the flowers and skies so bright.
Two years ago, I laid her there
With tears of penitence—a prayer
To God that, in the far Unknown,
She might forgive me. Pearl, I own

" I did not love my gifted wife,
Yet strove to make her wedded life
A happy one.
          Lulena cared
Alone for art. Her father shared
Her confidence. Both won a *name*—
Lived less for *love* or *home* than FAME.

" Her works of sculpture grace to-day
The palaces of Rome. They say
' Rome's lost her brightest genius ;' yet
I loved her not.
          Dear Margaret,

My home is lonely.   Come to me
And bless my life, sweet Margarié.

" I marvel, nature richly blest .
As yours, can find true pleasure—rest
In friendship.
            Pearl, it can not be!
Please answer
            Yours, impatiently."

XI.

HER COMMENT.

Men think, like ripened fruits on boughs unshaken,
Our love is waiting.

             They're oft mistaken!

XII.

PEARL'S ANSWER.

ᵞOU have marveled what pleasure, what true hap-
    piness
  Mere friendship can give to a woman like me ;
Or, one fitted to taste the delirious bliss
  Of loving, perhaps being loved, tenderly ?

ᵞou remember my joy on a balmy June eve
  In days long ago, as we sat by the sea,
Sang and studied the sunset ?   I never will grieve
  If hours of such happiness oft come to me.

Paul, have you forgotten that fair summer day
  We rode through the dreamy old forest so free ?
Did we envy the happy wood-robins their lay,
  As we climbed the steep cliffs hand in hand ?
      To me

Twas a joy more complete than my senses had
    known.
  I dreamed not of *love ;* knew the hour could not
    last ;

That our paths would diverge, that again I, alone,
 Must climb those bald cliffs as I had in the past.

And one night, while we sailed o'er the moonlighted
  bay,
 You whispered, so softly, these words in my ear—
Ah, they thrill my soul yet !—" Pearl, my darling
  alway
 I'll keep in remembrance my pupil so dear."

Still, *forgot me*, ere golden October had fled ;
 Then, phantom-like Doubt tore the thin veil away
From my heart, that so long, aye, so gladly, had fed
 On poor husks of friendship *I offer* to-day.

" She was cold, could not love," you have said of
  the *dead*
 Lulena—and, Leighton, perhaps it was true—
But you know there's a mountain called Hecla
  whose head
 Is wrapped in a hood of perpetual snow.

Far below that cold mask do they find ice and snow
 Or lava floods surging and seething, alone ?
Paul, some women are Heclas ; God help them
  for oh,
 Their hearts cry for bread, yet receive but "
  stone !"

No.   To take for my king, for my guiding star here,
  A nature as weak, or more fickle than mine,
'Twould blot out sun and moon from my sky,
      bright and clear,
  And make life a burden.

                              Adieu.   Ever thine.   ,

XIII.

OLD LETTERS.

THE clock is striking from the tower,
The time is "midnight's holy hour."

Alone, beside her desk she stands,
An open letter in her hands,

And reads, while tears bedim her eyes :
" Dear Margarié : " oh, glad surprise !

" Before I go away again,
  I'll cowardly allow my pen

" To tell you how a vulture tears
  My heart to-night with grief. Two years

" Ago, I met, in lovely Rome,
  Lulena Snover, in her home

" Of taste and wealth and art combined ;
  An Artist's home, where mind met mind.

(39)

" There, in that happy atmosphere
　　Of music, flowers, and pictures rare,

" Helped by her father's patronage
　　My poor attempts became the rage.

" ' Lulena's portrait you must try,'
　　Her father said, ' and, by-the-by,

" ' The dear girl chooses *you*,' said he,
　　' Of all the artists here, you see.'

" Lulena's picture grew apace,
　　From out the canvas gleamed a face

" As full of pride, passion, and power,
　　As Juno's ; and, O, evil hour !

" (She is my senior years full ten)
　　I sought this paragon again.

" I won Lulene, and thought with pride
　　That I could love my artist bride,

" Dearer than aught in life or art ;
　　But, Pearl, I did not know my heart.

" My health was failing.　Northern air
　　And rest from labor, thought, and care

" I found, and, with them—ah, too late !
    My life's *ideal.* Cruel fate !

" Sweet Margarié, my pearl most fair,
    I love you. Child, your waving hair

" Is dearer far than Lulu's gold—
    Her genius, fame, and beauty cold.

" Alas, in honor I am bound
    To wed Lulene ! A grief profound

" Is mine to-night. Adieu—but yet,
    Believe me, lovely Margaret,

" If I to win your love were free,
    To kiss your cheeks, sweet Margarié,

" And watch their color come and go,
    Like roses on a bank of snow,

" And hold your dainty hand in mine,
    'Twould be a joy almost divine.

" But Fate divides us. Angels bright
    Guard all your future. Pearl, good-night !

" I dare not trust my fickle heart
    To *say* ' Good-bye,' before we part ;

" Yet while I live, a golden dream
These dear, dead summer days will seem.

" Your gift of daisies, pure and white,
Sweet *Marguerites*, plucked to-night

" By you, a *souvenir* till death
I'll keep, and kiss with latest breath."

XIV.

THE REASON WHY.

THE Lady Pearl for all the seven years,
Kissed it, and laid it by with falling tears;

Then, from another yellow paper, read:
" My Daughter Margaret:—Last night Paul said:

" ' Dear Earl, pray give this parting note to Pearl
As soon as I have gone away. Sweet girl,

" ' I know she'll mourn my absence, for an hour,
Then turn, with girlish zest, to book and flower

" ' For pleasure; while, in haste, alas! I fly
From her enchantments dear. My Lord, good-
    bye!'

' He wrung my hand again, with grief sincere,
And quickly left the Hall. A sudden fear—

(43)

" I beg your pardon, child—made it seem best
   That you should think him cruel till the last ;

" Hoping his cold neglect would quickly prove
   An antidote to this, your fancied love.

" May lover come not till a far-off day
   To steal my Pearl, my darling Queen, away."

.   .   .   .   .   .

Yes, though full seven years had drifted by
Since both were penned, Pearl gave this joyous
   cry :
" Dear God, I thank Thee !   At this distant day
Paul does not know I threw my heart away ! "

And with this knowledge came the olden joy,
Her youthful faith unmixed with Doubt's alloy.

" To-morrow morn I'll lay my pride aside—
   Obey my heart—and tell him that his bride

" I'd rather be, than sit upon a throne
   And *rule the* WORLD.   My new-born love will
      own,"

She said, with burning blushes, streaming eyes,
Then read the missives o'er with new surprise.

The morning came at *last*.   She found that Paul,
Without *adieux*, at dawn, had left the Hall.

" My faith and penitence have come too late ;
I've killed his love ! " she said.   Ah, cruel fate !

XV.

A WINTER.

WEARILY, slowly, the days crept along;
No gayety, laughter, music, or song
Enlivened the Hall that whole winter long.

Snow drifted over the graves in the Park,
Still was the Hall as a vault and as dark ;
Yet, to its mistress, a sheltering ark.

Margaret, wrapped in a sorrowful dream,
White and as mute as the statues that gleam
Life-like and pure 'mid the trees in the sheen

Of silvery moonbeams. Closed was the Hall
To neighbors and friends, acquaintances, all ;
For Feeling seemed numb—Hope under a pall.

(47)

Life was a meaningless void.   Day and night
On sorrow and death—her love's early blight—
Dwelt her lone heart, once so joyous and light.

She dreaded the future, sighed for the past ;
Lived in the days that, for her, could not last !
Unheeding the present, flying so fast.

Oh, had her dear, dead young mother from o'er
The river of Death, its echoless shore,
Beheld sweet Margaret Malley once more ;

Pitying tears would have fallen, I know ;
If angels can weep for sorrows below ;
Or for Niobes whose tears can not flow.

You've seen the sun set in the sea, I trow ;
Or into an ocean of mist sink low,
And old Night swoop down over all below ?

Stretch his still dark wings o'er the land so brigh
Of late, and Day fade into darksome night ?
Well, so had Joy's sunshine taken its flight !

    .   .   .   .   .   .

Since, from the Hall had journeyed far away
The artist ; in her thoughts both night and day
The letter found had lived—a sacred lay.

Ah, this so-called love is a mystery
Strange and fathomless, as is *life* to me,
Or the endless years of eternity.

Thus, like daily tides and the sun's red gold,
Is my story new to the young, but old
To many—ay, e'en like *a tale twice told.*

XVI.

COMPANY.

WITH hawthorn bloom and birds of May
The Countess of Allaine one day

Came with her son Allaine's proud Earl,
She said, to cheer the Lady Pearl.

" Have just returned from France, my dear,
Where we have been almost a year.

" That you are lonely, child, we hear;
You know we both are friends sincere;"

She said, and, with a close embrace,
Rained kisses on the orphan's face.

Pearl's mother, born in far-off Maine,
Niece of the late Earl of Allaine,

Child of his only sister, fair
And stately Lady Alice Blair,

(51)

Who, on New England's surf-washed shore
Had found a grave, long years before.

At his request the orphaned May
To " Merry England ," far away

Went to the Earl, her uncle.   He
Called her a sacred legacy.

Her governess, Rose Lee, a true
New England girl, went with her, too,

To find a home—and not in vain—
For, soon the kind Earl of Allaine

Wedded the governess; and plain
Rose Lee became Lady Allaine.

Yet, ever after, strange to say,
Remained a friend to lovely May;

Rejoiced with all a mother's pride
When May became Lord Malley's bride;

And shed most bitter tears the day
Pearl's mother passed from earth away;

And vowed: " Sweet child ! dear motherless !
With my maternal love I'll bless,

" And wed thee to my son and heir."
Disinterested lady (!) " Fair

Queen Margaret " to London went
Last year.   To their dull parlors lent

Her lovely presence.   Lord Allaine,
Heir to the late Earl's vast domain,

Sought the young heiress; but, with pain,
Acknowledged he had wooed in vain ;

Still, more enamored grew, and sighed :
" This jewel yet shall be my bride."

.

XVII.

THE RECEPTION.

WELL, Pearl received her friends with joyless mien
  And smileless face, yet grand in its repose
As sweet day lilies sleeping, cold, serene
  As petals of an ice-imprisoned rose.

" More like a statue of herself, than Pearl,
  Or sleeper, moving in the moon-ray's gleam,"
The Countess sadly thought, " than the sweet girl
  Who last year graced my *soirées*." " Do I dream ? "

Sighed Lord Allaine, and quickly looked away
  To hide his deep surprise ; then mutely pressed
Her unresponsive fingers, longed to say :—
  "Oh, frozen Daisy, come to me and rest ! "

' This portly Earl Allaine, with pompous air,
  Chin dimpled, brow too low for genius—kind
Blue eyes, flushed face, blonde mustache, tawny hair;
  With lips too full for feelings quite refined,

" Or tastes æsthetic; has a heart as kind
   And tender as a woman's. He would prove
As true as gold to one, who with a blind,
   Unshrinking faith, could give him love for love,

" And hand for heart ; " instinctively his fair
   Young hostess thought, shuddered, then led the
      way
To parlors filled with light and perfumed air,
   Bright with anemones; exotics gay,—

Where ferns and ivies in rare vases, clung
   Or twined themselves in graceful beauty round
Choice paintings, marble goddesses, and hung
   From bronzes rich, and chalices gold-bound,

And silken lambrequins, and laces rare
   Artistically draped, or drawn aside,
To let the sunshine and the sweet May air
   Bless blooming plants; of late, her care and pride.

XVIII.

A PROPOSITION.

THE Countess soon declared that it was wrong
   For her dear kins-woman thus to immure
Herself within the grand old Hall so long;
   And strove, with thoughts of travel, to allure

Her mind from sorrow. Then proposed that she
   With her should cross the ocean—while away
The summer in Columbia, and see
   The grand Centennial. From day to day

Talked of the Exposition,—dwelt with pride
   On the improvements which a century
Had wrought,—of ancestors who fought, ay, *died*,
   In gloomy forests, for sweet Liberty.

'Yes, Edward, I've been loyal to the Queen—
   Your father too! Through all my wedded years
Have scarcely dreamed of *home*. Yet, olden scenes
   Come back, to-night, and move my heart to tears.

" I've been an exile over thirty years
  From friends and haunts so loved in early days,
I long to see my Boston home—the dear
  Old South Church where, so oft, in songs of
    praise

" I joined my young companions, long ago.
  And, Pearl, your grandmother, the Lady Blair,
Lies in her lonesome grave in Maine. I know
  You'll visit it. The Earl erected there

" A monument which cost a thousand pounds.
  I well remember when she died ; how May,
Your darling mother, flung her arms around
  My neck, and begged me not to go away.

" But I am growing garrulous, I know—
  I beg your pardon, child—but promise me
That to this Exposition you will go,
  With Edward and myself, across the sea."

XVIX.

THE JOURNEY.

PEARL promised, and, in June, 'mid storm and cloud,
  They sailed across Atlantic's bosom wide—
First visited New England's cities proud,
  Then saw Mount Washington in all his pride.

Admired the perfect scenery around,
  Sailed on St. Lawrence past the " Thousand Isles,"
Soon stood with rapt delight, and gazed, spell-bound,
  Upon sublime Niagara the while.

Saw Canada—the Lakes—the South ; rode days
  O'er prairies green.   A thousand miles, or more,
Sailed on the Mississippi.   Steamed away
  Across the Continent.   The golden shore

Of far Pacific reached,—then, much amazed
  Plucked lush, ripe grapes from purple vineyards
      there.
Went to Yosemite, with wonder gazed
  Upon the Bridal Vail, the clear blue air

And mountain scenery, sublimely grand;
  Where snow-crowned summits kiss the clouds, rise
    high
Peak above peak—then sought the magic land
  Of mammoth trees whose branches cleave the sky

They journeyed eastward.   In the autumn days
  Reached the Centennial.   Lady Allaine
And titled son were lavish in their praise—
  Said :—" *To describe it all, is quite in vain !* "

" All expectation it exceeds.   To see
  This Exposition, dearest Margaret,
Through life a pleasant memory will be;
  To miss it, but a lifetime of regret ! "

The grounds with foliage and flowers were gay;
  Skies never brighter seemed.   From morn til
  ·   night
The three, like children on a holiday,
  Examined works of art with strange delight.

XX.

PEARL'S CONCLUSION.

PEARL hourly grew more cheerful
  As the summer days waxed long;
Her pallid lips, eyes tearful,
  Gave place to smile and song.
With health's warm roses, burning
  Once again on cheeks of snow,
Came spirits gay, returning
  Fraught with all their olden glow.

Lady Allaine was hopeful,
  Thought, with true maternal pride,
" The Earl will be successful;
  He will win his chosen bride."
Lord Edward was but human,
  He believed his lordly hand
Worthy the sweetest woman
  Whom he knew in all the land.

But, at the Exhibition,
  Pearl seemed far more sad than gay;

For art her old ambition
　　Would return, then die away.
At times, when fancy painted
　　All the lonesome, loveless years
To come, her tried heart fainted,
　　Though she still repressed her tears,

And thought, with strange emotion,
　　Lips and cheeks of ashen hue,
"For Lord Allaine's devotion
　　Some reward is surely due.
Yet, for his love so tender,
　　True respect and friendship kind
Are all that I can render.
　　Well, 'tis said that 'Love is blind.'

"That, two classes of lovers
　　Wise experience has proved,
Are found the whole world over—
　　'*Those who love* and *those beloved.*'
Although my heart can never
　　All alone to him be given ;
Or, such a marriage ever
　　Quite be blessed to me of heaven.

"Perhaps, 'tis best to sever
　　All connection with my past,
The Earl wed, and endeavor
　　To find *peace* and rest at last."

Alas, this sage conclusion
    Filled her heart and mind with pain ;
She thought, with strange confusion,
    " To *myself* I'll true remain."

" Although earth-ties, affections,
    Yes, husband and children dear
And all love's sweet protection
    Are through life denied me here ;
I'll find enough of beauty
    Still, in Nature, books, and art
To cheer me on in duty,
    Help me act a Christian's part."

Again, two careless lovers
    Walking arm in arm along,
Or young and happy mother
    Who, in all that surging throng
Of moving human beings,
    Saw alone her baby's face,
She met—or young bride seeing
    Smile and blush, with timid grace

Receive, in glad contentment,
    Words of praise, attentions kind,—
" Oh, Fates ! this sweet enchantment
    Once again fling 'round my mind,"

Sighed Pearl.   " Ah, to be treated
   Thus, with tenderness alway !
My wants anticipated
   With such loving care.   Each day

" Attentions kind receiving,
   Cheered by jest and laughter light,
Is better, far, than grieving
   O'er my perished hopes.   'Tis right
That I my *dead* should bury,
   Bid my gloomy thoughts adieu,
And, kind Lord Edward marry,
   For his love is warm and true."

XXI.

IN ART GALLERY.

WITHIN the Art Department, hour by hour,
With Earl Allaine ever beside her chair,
The Lady Margaret, in dire dismay,
Listened to whispered comments on the rare
Vases and paintings, statues, tapestry,
And rich mosaics in the Gallery.
   He talked of the exhibits from abroad,
Contrasted works of foreign art and ours
With such a painful lack of culture, taste,
Of fine discrimination, knowledge, power,
That his companion bit her rosy lips
With chagrin and disgust, I am afraid ;
Then turned away her face, in vain, to hide
The burning blushes dyeing neck and brow,
Called there by criticisms, quite unfair,
Upon the statuary gathered there.
Then, suddenly, " Look at this picture !" cried
The Earl ; " 'tis very finely done, indeed !
 I met the artist once, five years ago
In Rome ; was in his studio, and saw
This very painting there ; unfinished then."

PEARL.

She looked in silence, but his words recalled
From out the hidden crypts of buried hopes,
Features which she contrasted mentally
With her companion's heavy, florid face.
Saw Paul (a very prince amongst the men
Whom she had met abroad, also at home),
With keenest ear for music, eye for art,
Love for esthetics, and soul all alert
With power to understand, appreciate
All nature ; and capacities so great
For loving the sublime and beautiful.
His bearing elegant—a soul-lit face
So eloquent with feeling, grand with thought ;
A noble forehead crowned with midnight hair,
And eyes so dark and glorious, when fired
By genius, love, or sympathy.   Lips proud,
But delicate.   A sweet and winning smile.
Contrasted well *his* face with Earl Allaine's—
A lump of coarser clay—though kind and true,
The animal predominating there,
O'ershadowing both intellect and soul.
" The contrast is too great between the Earl
And artist," sadly mused the Lady Pearl.
    That night she dreamed of Paul. So vivid seeme
The vision, that the morning's rosy rays
Could not dispel his image from her thoughts.
His presence permeated all the air.
If there are brain waves, surely this was one.
Is there an atmosphere around each soul

Like that enveloping our earth?   Or have
The parts we call immortal—soul and mind,
Surrounding antennæ invisible?
Or strange electric currents, sensitive
To slightest contact with the sentient waves
Of brain enveloping approaching friends,
Sending a thrill of strange expectancy,
Of feeling like a rising tidal wave,
Or longing to behold the face and form
Of one we love, submerging Reason quite ;
Making us dream, foreshadowing events
To come, until we blindly stretch our arms—
These antennæ of soul and sense—to kiss
And fold the unseen living presence dear
In an embrace sweeter than sense of touch,
Causing a thrill of rapture, or of pain,
Or terrible suspense?   The startling, keen
Impression that Calamity is near,
Which comes to us, at times, in sleeping hours,
But quite as often in our *waking* dreams?
Or are we warned by angels?   Do they touch
Us with their spirit hands invisible?
Or whisper in our ears predictions true?
Oh, learnéd students in psychology,
Or, sage philosophers, pray answer me!

XXII.

A MEETING.

THEY were strolling one day in the Park, side by
    side, ·
  "Dearest Pearl," said the Earl, "I am waiting to
    hear
From your lips life or death to my hopes—be my
    bride—
  Cheer and brighten my home with your presence
    so dear.

'The Countess, my good mother, loves you like a
    child,   ·
  My first, last, *only* LOVE; let me call you '*my*
    PEARL,'"
But, withdrawing her hand, Lady Pearl quickly
    smiled,
  Crimsoned, and then grew white as the dying.
    The Earl

Saw a stranger approaching, and felt that the twain
  Had loved dearly—their faces, instinct with new
    life,

Told him that they loved still—and, in anger and
    pain,
    He knew well sweet Pearl Malley would ne'er be
    his wife.

Yet he reddened and stared, and his eyes fairly
    burned,
    While Paul Leighton shook hands with the lady
    again ;
(For Paul read in her eyes that his love was re-
    turned).
    When the Earl of Allaine, though the mildest
    of men,

Bowed with courtly politeness and held out his
    hand,
    For he recognized Paul, as an artist from Rome.
Then he said : " Lady Pearl," in a tone of command,
    " Come, the phaeton's here ; we must turn to-
    ward home."

" I will see you to-morrow," said Paul, as the twain
    Bowled away through the beautiful Park in the
    glow
Of the glorious sunset. Pearl told Lord Allaine
    Of her love for the artist. " I wish you to know

Why I can not be yours, my dear Cousin Allaine,
    For I owe you much kindly attention. For years

have tried to forget him—to love *you*—in vain ;
Yet forgive me," still urged her brown eyes, wet
  with tears.

Will I pardon you ?   Yes.   'Twas my fault.
  Dearest girl,
May your future be peaceful, your life glad and
  bright ;
May God bless you and keep you !   Farewell,
  darling Pearl,
For I leave the ' Centennial City ' to-night ! "

XXIII.

LORD EDWARD.

QUICKLY fell the Countess' tears
When she found the hopes of years
    All had fled ;
But, the courtly Lord Allaine
Deftly hiding his heart-pain,
    Quickly said :

" No, my mother, you must stay
Till you give the bride away,
    For, you know,
None will chaperone our dear
Margaret—a stranger here—
    If *you* go?

" Yes, 'tis true, she was my choice,
But, the Lady Edith Boise
    Still is free ;
And, you know, before she went
Last year, to the Continent,
    Cared for *me*.

" Though for lovely Pearl, to-day,
  Sore in heart I go away,
            Mother dear ;
  Lady Edith I may find,
  If not quite so fair, more kind.
            Dry your tears

" And, in Paris, I'll forget,
  If I can, ' Queen Margaret '—
            Strive to win
  Charming Edith, for my bride,
  Ere the happy Christmas tide
            Shall begin."

Smile not, oh, my reader true !
Though, his fickleness to *you*
            May seem rare ;
For, in *real life*, I ween,
Constancy (?) like this is seen,
            Critic fair,

And, in *love-life* we have found
Hearts are won in the " re-bound."
            And, 'tis true,
One in *pique* may win a wife,
But, alas ! long years of strife
            May ensue.

XXIV.

TO PEARL.

PEARL :—

If I've read your eyes aright?
Wear these daisies, in the morning,
Wavy, gold-brown hair adorning
    With my bridal daisies white ;
    Yours, with *all* Paul's love ; Good-night.

XXV.

TO PAUL.

PAUL:—

    Marguerites " pure and white "—
" Bridal daisies," sent to-night
With your love, my life to brighten,
I will wear with joy, dear Leighton.
    Yours, with *all* Pearl's love ; Good-night.

XXVI.

MORNING.

ALL thy rays, O Sun, are beaming
  With delight.   Autumnal flowers
And the tinted leaves are dreaming
  With a joy, new born.   The Hours

Sing and laugh—rehearse the glory
  O'er and o'er of Eden days—
Earth's first lovers—tell the story
  To the list'ning Air ablaze

With a hazy, mellow splendor.
  Oh, these dreamy purple skies,
Blending with the blue and tender
  Mists, which from the Schuylkill rise!

" All the world is full of beauty,
  Eden joys and blooming bowers;
And, again, sweet Love and Duty
  Bid me wear these snowy flowers.

(79)

" They recall the dear lost pleasures
 Of my past—its summer hours—
.Somewhere, still, among my treasures
 Is a bunch of withered flowers,

" Which, Paul wreathed amid my tresses;
 Gifts, my heart taught me to prize
More than all the Malley diamonds.
 Far more precious in my eyes

" Are these daisies; " said her tender,
 Smiling lips of ruby hue,
Sweet, brown eyes with youthful splendor
 Beaming. Joy to Pearl was *new*.

XXVII.

AT LAST.

WHY repeat the old, old story
　　　How the twain
In the Autumn's golden glory
　　　Met again?

Of the voiceless rapture filling
　　　Heart and brain,
Soul as well as senses thrilling?
　　　Tongue and pen

Weakly falter while repeating
　　　Bliss like theirs;
For, we see, in such a meeting,
　　　Answered prayers.

On a glad November morning,
　　　O'er the sea,
Bridal white her form adorning
　　　Margarie

Wedded Paul with joy bells ringing
From the tower,
Round which ivy-green is clinging,
Blissful hour!

And, while wedding bells are chiming
With delight;
Reader, I will cease my rhyming—
Say " Good-night."

www.ingramcontent.com/pod-product-compliance
Lightning Source LLC
Chambersburg PA
CBHW022140090426
42742CB00010B/1338